Animals of the Night

COYOTES
AFTER DARK

Heather M. Moore Niver

Enslow Publishing
101 W. 23rd Street
Suite 240
New York, NY 10011
USA

enslow.com

Words to Know

burrow—A hole or den made into a home by a small animal.

carnivores—Animals that eat meat.

extinct—Not existing or active any longer.

habitats—Places in which animals live.

mammals— Animals that have a backbone and hair, usually give birth to live babies, and produce milk to feed their young.

nocturnal—Mostly active at night.

pack—A group of animals, usually wild, that live together, such as coyotes or wolves.

prey—An animal hunted by another animal for food.

prowling—Moving about quietly and secretly.

stalking—Watching and following prey from a distance.

Contents

On the Prowl

The sun sets after a long, hot day. The **nocturnal** coyote has a busy night ahead. She has rested all day. Now she is ready to hunt for food for her family. She begins **prowling** through the fields during the cooler, darker hours. She has babies to feed, so she is not picky.

With only the moonlight to guide her, the coyote sniffs the air. She catches the scent of a mouse in the tall grass. She hunches down and stays perfectly still. Then she pounces! Now she has a snack for her hungry pups.

FUN FACT!

Coyotes are a main character in many Native American stories. They are often very smart, creative beasts in the stories, but sometimes they are a bit silly, too.

Coyotes are well known for their classic howls in the night. Many times they are shown in the movies and stories as lonely figures howling at a full moon.

Classic Coyote

Coyotes are **mammals** that look a lot like dogs.
This is because they are wild members of the dog family.
They are smaller and lighter than wolves. Coyotes are
sometimes called by different names. They may be called
prairie wolf or brush wolf. A California wildlife expert
calls them "ghost dogs" because they can live so close to
humans without being seen.

FUN FACT!

Coyotes are not the only wild
members of the dog family.
Foxes, jackals, coyotes, and
dogs all belong to a family
called *canid*.

Coyotes like to spend a lot of their time alone, but they also live in packs with several other coyotes.

Most coyotes are about 2 feet (60 centimeters) tall at their shoulders. They are about 3 to 4 feet (about a meter) long, including the tail. An adult coyote weighs about 20 to 50 pounds (9 to 23 kilograms). The largest ones usually live in the northeastern United States and Canada.

Coyotes have long rough fur that is usually a mix of gray and brown. They have some white on their stomachs and throats. Coyotes may have reddish fur on their legs. Their tails are thick and fluffy. Sometimes there is a black tip on the tail.

FUN FACT!

Male coyotes are often larger than females.

A coyote's multicolored coat helps it blend in with its environment, which helps to make it a better hunter.

Coyotes have been on earth since the Ice Age. That's about 20,000 years! Ice Age coyotes were a bit different from those we see prowling around today. They were much larger and stronger. At the time, they were competing against other larger animals, such as wolves, for **prey**. Coyotes had bigger teeth and larger jaws, too. Scientists think this is because these **carnivores** needed big, sharp teeth to cut and tear their meat. Their prey was big, too. They ate horses and camels.

Little by little, coyotes became smaller after their large prey and large competitors went **extinct**.

Where in the World?

Coyotes once lived in open areas such as prairies and deserts. Today they live all over most of the United States and Canada, as well as Central America. Coyotes can also now be found in habitats such as mountains and forests. They may even make their homes in populated areas like New York, Chicago, or Houston. Sometimes they even live in large parks.

Although records show cases of coyotes attacking humans, it is very rare. Most of the time coyotes are afraid of humans and avoid them. But they learn to live nearby.

Coyotes have learned to make themselves at home in cities and other areas with lots of humans. This coyote is walking through Griffith Park in Los Angeles, California.

Clever, Smart, and Speedy

Coyotes are smart and can live in all kinds of habitats. One reason is because they will eat almost anything. Sometimes coyotes will hunt deer or farm animals, such as calves and lambs. Mice and voles are often on the coyote menu, and they will also snack on lizards, snakes, or insects. If they get very hungry they will look through human garbage to get a snack. Coyotes will do whatever it takes to survive. And it works, because the population of coyotes is healthy and successful.

FUN FACT!

Coyotes change their hunting style based on what food is available. They hunt small prey alone, but work with other coyotes to catch larger animals.

Coyotes usually eat small mammals, such as rabbits, squirrels, and mice.

Coyotes are known for their speed as well as their smarts. Most of the time they walk or jog. But when they need to, they can chase after prey at 40 miles (64 km) per hour. These great hunters can also jump up to 13 feet (4 m) high. A coyote on its own might travel in an area up to 60 square miles (about 97 sq km).

They are not very good at climbing, but coyotes are very good swimmers. They can swim distances up to half a mile (almost one kilometer).

When prey is in sight, coyotes can put on a burst of speed to make sure they catch their next meal.

Super Senses

Coyotes are fantastic hunters. Their super senses of sight, smell, and hearing help them out. Coyotes have excellent eyesight for spotting prey. More importantly, coyotes use their eyesight to communicate. They carefully watch the expressions and body language of other members of their **pack**.

Coyotes have a sharp sense of smell that helps them sniff out their next meal. And their keen sense of hearing helps them scout out the tiniest animals.

FUN FACT!

Coyotes communicate without a word. They can "read" one another's body language, just like humans. They can see if another coyote is angry or playful, just by how they hold their body.

Coyotes communicate in many ways. Sound and body language are only two ways. They also sniff each other, lick, nip, bite, and even jump.

Coyotes have their own way of hunting. When they are "mousing," they sniff out a mouse or other prey while **stalking** through the grass. Once a mouse is spotted, the coyote stops and crouches, perfectly still. Then it pounces! It's time for dinner.

When coyotes hunt in groups for larger animals, they take turns chasing the animal until the prey gets tired. Sometimes several of them chase the animal and drive it to another hidden coyote that attacks.

FUN FACT!

Badgers and coyotes might work together to hunt. Badgers are slow but can dig out mice. Coyotes aren't as good at digging but have the speed to catch the mouse.

Coyotes hunt small prey alone or in pairs, but they work in groups for larger meals, such as deer.

No Place Like Home

Most of the time, coyotes sleep above ground. They may sleep out in the open or under cover. Coyotes make their homes in dens when they have babies. Sometimes they dig their own homes in the ground. They might also make themselves at home in a **burrow**, or den, once belonging to a woodchuck or a badger. They dig to make that existing den bigger to fit their families. Coyotes may use their dens for a few years. Sometimes they make their dens in hollow tree stumps or between large rocks.

Coyotes like dens where they can see all around and watch for danger.

Coyotes usually have about six babies, or pups, in April or May. But they can have between one and nineteen pups. A group of baby pups is called a litter. Coyote pups are born blind and cannot see for the first eleven or twelve days. They live in the den with their mother and feed on her milk.

After about six weeks the pups begin to explore the world outside the den. They also start to eat prey that their mother and father bring back for them.

FUN FACT!

Male pups usually leave the den and go off on their own after six to nine months. Females often stay with their parents and form a pack.

Most coyote pups are hunting on their own by the fall.

Howling and Yelping

Because they are so active at night, coyotes need to use sound to communicate in the dark. They use all kinds of sounds, including growls, bark-howls, whines, and yelps. When you hear a group of coyotes howling or yip-howling, they are letting other coyotes know where they live. This helps family members find them, too. Coyotes might yelp when they are playing. Parents make a huffing sound to tell their pups to come to them.

FUN FACT!

Coyotes communicate silently by leaving their scent behind. They may mark an area with their urine to let others know the area is claimed.

Coyotes make a variety of sounds: from howls to barks, yips, growls, snorts, and even snapping their teeth.

Top Dog

In general, coyotes do not have any predators. Sometimes larger carnivores, such as bears, wolves, and mountain lions will hunt small young pups. Very occasionally, coyotes will attack and kill one another.

In most cases, human hunters and motor vehicles such as cars or tractors cause many coyote deaths every year. But a coyote's most likely cause of death is from a disease, such as a skin illness called mange, which causes the coyote's fur to fall out and its skin to itch uncontrollably.

Coyotes are so smart that in areas with many vehicles, they figured out that they should not cross a street before looking left and right.

Stay Safe
Around Coyotes

Coyotes often live near people, but that's no reason to worry. There are some simple steps you can take to make sure everyone—you and the coyotes—can live together peacefully and safely.

 Never feed coyotes.

Keep bird food, pet food, ripe fruit, and garbage in areas where a coyote cannot get to it.

Pet lovers can protect their furry friends from coyotes by feeding the pet only in the house and keeping it inside at night.

 Fencing can keep pets and small farm animals like chickens safe. Keep an eye on them when they are outside if you know coyotes have been on the prowl nearby. Fencing can also keep coyotes out. Make sure it is at least 4 feet (1.2 m) high.

Never try to remove a coyote on your own. Call an expert to do it properly.

If you see a coyote, don't try to run away. Wave your arms up in the air and try to look as big as possible. If that doesn't work, try throwing something at it. These actions might scare it off.

Learn More

Books

Linde, Barbara. *Coyotes and Wolves Are Not Pets!* New York: Gareth Stevens Learning, 2013.

Llanas, Sheila Griffin. *Coyotes*. Minneapolis: ABDO Publishing Company, 2013.

Read, Tracey C. *Exploring the World of Coyotes*. Buffalo, NY: Firefly Books, 2011.

Roza, Greg. *Your Neighbor the Coyote*. New York: Windmill Books, 2011.

Websites

National Geographic
kids.nationalgeographic.com/animals/coyote/
Learn more about coyotes with photos, maps, and more.

University of Michigan
biokids.umich.edu/critters/Canis_latrans/
Check out this website for facts, statistics, and more information about coyotes.

San Diego Zoo
kids.sandiegozoo.org/animals/mammals/coyote
Readers will learn a lot at this website with loads of photographs and facts about coyotes.

Index

Published in 2016 by Enslow Publishing, LLC.
101 W. 23rd Street, Suite 240, New York, NY 10011

Copyright © 2016 by Enslow Publishing, LLC.

Library of Congress Cataloging-in-Publication Data

Niver, Heather Moore, author.
 Coyotes after dark / Heather M. Moore Niver.
  pages cm. — (Animals of the night)
Audience: Ages 8+
Audience: Grades 4 to 6.
 Summary: "Describes the habits and nature of coyotes at night"— Provided
by publisher.
 Includes bibliographical references and index.
 ISBN 978-0-7660-7183-4 (library binding)
 ISBN 978-0-7660-7181-0 (pbk.)
 ISBN 978-0-7660-7182-7 (6-pack)
 1. Coyote—Behavior—Juvenile literature. 2. Coyote—Juvenile literature.
I. Title.
 QL737.C22N577 2016
 599.77'25—dc23
             2015026944

Printed in the United States of America

To Our Readers: We have done our best to make sure all website
addresses in this book were active and appropriate when we went to
press. However, the author and the publisher have no control over and
assume no liability for the material available on those websites or on any
websites they may link to. Any comments or suggestions can be sent by
e-mail to customerservice@enslow.com.

Photos Credits: Throughout book, narvikk/E+/Getty Images (starry
background), kimberrywood/Digital Vision Vectors/Getty Images
(green moon dingbat); cover, p. 1 sebartz/Shutterstock.com (coyote),
samxmed/E+/Getty Images (moon); p. 3 Tom Brakefield/Stockbyte/
Thinkstock; p. 5 © Design Pics Inc/Alamy; p. 7 prisma/SuperStock;
p. 9 Joshua Haviv/Shutterstock.com; p. 11 Matt Knoth/Shutterstock.
com; p. 13 David McNew/Getty Images News/Getty Images; p. 15
Gail Shumway/The Images bank/Getty Images; p. 17 Preston Hones/
Moment/Getty Images; p. 19 Fuse/Thinkstock; p. 21 Photography by
Gary Potts/Shutterstock.com; p. 23 Bob Bennett/Photodisc/Getty
Images; p. 25 Design Pics/David Ponton/Stockbyte/Getty Images;
p. 27 Danita Delimont/Gallo Images/Getty Images; p. 29 Michael
Sewell/Photolibrary/Getty Images.